EFT- BEST PRACTICES
For ENERGY MANAGEMENT

EFT- BEST PRACTICES For ENERGY MANAGEMENT

===========

How to Reap Optimal Benefits From Your EFT & Energy Therapy Sessions

ANNE I. MERKEL, PH.D., CNHP

**The Ariela Group Publications
- Mineral Bluff - Georgia**

Copyright ©2015   Anne I. Merkel, Ph.D., CNHP

ALL RIGHTS RESERVED. No part of this book may be reproduced in any way without prior written permission from the author, Anne Merkel. Appropriate citations should be included with any reference to said information.

The author of this book does not dispense medical advice nor prescribe the use of any technique as a form of treatment for physical, emotional, or medical problems without the advice of a physician, either directly or indirectly. In the event that you use any of the information in this book for yourself, the author and the publisher assume no responsibility for your actions.

ISBN: 978-0-9961262-1-2

Join us at these locations to learn more about our Energy Therapy Programs!

Coaching Services : www.ArielaGroup.com

Alchemist Anne Blog: www.AlchemistAnne.com

My EFT Coach Blog: www.MyEFTCoach.com

EFT & Energy Therapy Mastermind Groups:

   www.arielagroup.com/mastermind

Practitioner Training & Certification:

   www.arielagroup.com/goingdeeper

"We Inspire Conscious Living and Guide Transformation in individuals and organizations who desire to re-access the natural state of Pure Potentiality!"

CONTENTS

This book presents some of the "behind-the-scenes" aspects of Meridian Tapping Techniques such as EFT, and:

- explains why Meridian Tapping Techniques work,
- describes why they don't work sometimes,
- shares how to best access your subconscious so that it will pay attention to you, and
- lists some beneficial after-session "clean up" techniques that will speed up the results you feel from your EFT or Energy Therapy session.

Contents	**Page 5**
Preface	**Page 7**
Introduction	**Page 9**
What is Energy Therapy?	**Page 13**
Who Needs Energy Therapy?	**Page 18**
Accessing the Subconscious	**Page 27**
Using the EFT Set-Up Statement	**Page 32**
When Techniques Don't Work	**Page 36**
The Body's Priorities	**Page 40**

Nurturing Your Subconscious   **Page 43**
Energy Clearing   **Page 52**
Dispelling the Energetic "Ash"   **Page 54**
Resources   **Page 58**

PREFACE

My journey toward writing this book started many years ago when I decided that my passion was in facilitating and teaching others to use energy therapies. I decided that I would share with others the many tools that I continue to use to clear my own system of blockages so that I can be a clear channel for the work that I do.

This short book, and a series of others, are my gift to you and all of those others who are searching for a better, easier, faster way to move with the natural energy flow and clear all resistance and blockage along the way.

This particular book will point out certain nuances or "Best Practices" for Energy Management that I have learned through many years of study and application of many modalities. It is a perfect support guide for any EFT Practitioner either just getting started or wanting to amp up a practice.

I am grateful that you have joined me on this journey to healing – of yourself and others, via improving your own understanding and processing of energy therapy techniques. Please let me know how I can be of further service to you!!

Also, you may wish to sign up for my e-book **Ten Keys to Pure Potentiality**, found on my website.[1]

---

[1] To obtain this e-book go to: http://arielagroup.com

INTRODUCTION

During thirty years of formal and informal post-doctorate training, I have actively pursued and facilitated multiple energy therapy modalities. Following a path from simple hands-on healing as a child, to Healing Touch, Shaman Journeying, Reiki Master-hood, Touch for Health, color and sound therapies, Neuro Linguistic Programming, Applied Kinesiology, energetic removal techniques, Neuro Emotional Technique/NET, and Emotional Freedom Technique/EFT, I have facilitated thousands of cases for clients world-wide. I am blessed to have been invited as a healing agent by these wonderful souls, and I am also blessed to be able to facilitate such potent modalities as those in my energetic toolbox.

I appreciate Dr. Scott Walker and Dr. Deb Walker, with whom I continue to study advanced Neuro Emotional Technique, Neuro Emotional Extra Techniques, and Neuro Emotional Anti-sabotage Techniques. I am grateful to their research and the continuing evolution of NET. And, I am grateful for the scientific research work being done through NET

Mind Body and The One Foundation to alert more physicians and health practitioners of this powerful approach to healing the mind, body, and spirit.[2]

I am thankful to Gary Craig for putting other techniques together to create Emotional Freedom Techniques. I appreciate that he and his daughter Tina continue to keep their standards very high as the world of EFT continues to grow.[3]

Most practitioners of EFT are unaware of the earliest connection of EFT with the field of chiropractic and applied kinesiology. EFT was developed as a third generation modality beyond Dr. George Goodheart's original findings about the energetic wiring of the body.[4] Blended with the ancient premises of acupuncture and acupressure both John Carragan of Thought Field Therapy/TFT[5] and Dr. Scott Walker of

---

[2] For more information visit: https://www.netmindbody.com/for-patients/an-explanation-of-net
[3] For more information visit: http://emofree.com
[4] For more information visit: http://www.icakusa.com/faqs and check "How did applied kinesiology start?"
[5] For more information visit: http://www.rogercallahan.com

Neuro Emotional Technique/NET[6] developed energetic protocols that combined specific tapping formulae that related to clearing specific emotional patterns.

I first studied and began using NET with clients. That was until I needed a simpler tool that I could apply on myself, and then I discovered EFT, which Gary Craig developed from TFT. In my own practice I generally blend a variety of modalities, and generally I apply N-hanced EFT (NET + EFT)[7] with my distance (by-phone) clients while I facilitate NET and other hands-on energy therapy modalities with face-to-face cases. All of my clients learn classic EFT to use on their own between sessions with me.

It is my intention here in this book to provide you with some advanced insights that will support your own study and practice of various energy modalities. As you go deeper into your own applications you will find that the tips I present here will support your success.

---

[6] For more information visit: http://netmindbody.com
[7] For more information visit: http://arielagroup.com/eft-net

I am always happy to answer any questions you might have or discuss how you can better integrate energy therapy modalities into your practice or your personal life. Feel free to contact me at: *info@arielagroup.com* and I'll be sure to respond.

WHAT IS ENERGY THERAPY?

Energy Therapy modalities center around the more subtle energies that can be best discerned via the right frontal lobe and central and lower limbic brain areas rather than rationalized and discussed through the analyzing left brain. Based on current studies and experience I'm convinced that more change can be facilitated via the right mind, subconscious, physiology, and energy field around the body than can ever be shifted through verbal analysis of the left brain! And, current neuroscience studies are even beginning to question the old right-left hemisphere theories as more is now known about how memories, energy, and emotions are held through-out the body and travel through all of the major physiological systems as well as the energetic meridian system.

It is generally thought that our right brain perceives the big picture and recognizes that everything is made up of energy particles that are universally connected. Since everything is connected, there is an intimate relationship between the atomic space around and within all beings. On an energetic level, if

I think about you, send good vibrations your way, pray for you, hold you in the Light, then I am consciously sending energy to you with my healing or positive intention. If I perform Reiki or Healing Touch or even lay my hands on you with intentions of healing, there will be results that modern quantum science is just beginning to understand. Our left brain and science have not yet caught up with what we naturally understand to be true about how our subconscious, biofields, and right hemispheres function.

The connection of the mind and body and spirit is undeniable and is just beginning to be understood. Studies of the balance of our left and right brain frontal lobe hemispheres is profound and starting to tap into how we learn to control and manage our thoughts, feelings, and as a result, create our destinies. Using this information and applying it while accessing the body's electro-magnetic biofield goes well beyond traditional therapies limited by their connection with the analytical mind. The use of energy modalities to communicate with the subconscious and make potent neuro-physical suggestions to our right mind and limbic brain is taking the field of psychology by storm.

Acupuncture and acupressure have been used effectively in cultures world-wide for thousands of years. They were finally accepted as beneficial by the AMA (American Medical Association) when it was hard to deny the efficacy of their use based on success cases, and when the evidence of energetic pathways or meridians was actually proven via the western medicine "scientific" electro-magnetic imagining devices. Now with communication and travel on the planet connecting all cultures and traditions, the cross-pollination is proving that one culture or discipline doesn't have to understand everything from another in order to accept that something works effectively. And, in brain talk, that simply means that just because the left brain (of society) cannot analyze and dissect and understand all aspects of a technique or process doesn't mean that its benefits won't be accepted and utilized by the right brain subconscious (public).

I often tell my clients or people in my audiences that they don't have to believe in or understand the tools that I use. I am talking to their subconscious minds and that part of them is able to talk back, make changes, and help the analytical minds to feel better... without needing to understand.

"Energy Therapy" and "Energy Psychology"[8] are terms that are becoming popularly used now to encompass many modalities that are used alone or as complementary therapy to traditional practices. Now coaches, therapists, physicians, and other health and wellness practitioners are eager to learn how to go more deeply into the root cause or energetic underlying cause of outer dis-ease to clear it. And usually these modalities are non-invasive, painless, quick, and relatively easy to facilitate. Some, like EFT, are easy to learn for self-application, while others require a facilitator to be most effective.

---

[8] For more information visit:
http://www.energypsych.org/?AboutEPv2

The fact that these therapies focus on shifting, neutralizing, or clearing energies, charges, or emotional blockages using a very short process that involves the body and its electro-magnetic field, and without requiring in-depth discussion about the issue, sets them aside from traditional psychology-based talk-therapies. These "energy-based" therapies don't require "the story", but instead ask the client being served to focus on feelings elicited by emotions in the present or past. The intention is to change neuro-pathways naturally rather than via repetitive manipulation, and the results can be profound.

WHO NEEDS ENERGY THERAPY?

In the energy model of health that I studied there are three main categories into which people fit when they present to physicians and therapists with pain, discomfort, stress, issues. These three categories are: **1-structural, 2-chemical & nutritional, 3-emotional.** They are all connected.

What this says is that in 99% of all cases of people feeling "sick" or being diagnosed with symptoms of dis-ease, stress, illness, they are suffering from one of the following:

- **Structural/infrastructure problems**: brought on through accident, fall, cut, sprain, strain, subluxation, etc.
- **Chemical & Nutritional imbalance**: brought on by food allergies & reactions, drugs, chemical combining, hormonal imbalance, diet creating unhealthy pH levels, imbalanced internal chemistry, ingestion of toxins, etc.

- **Emotional issues**: brought on through trauma, emotional experience, birth, life, DNA coding, etc.

The concept behind this approach is that when people present to a physician with pain of some kind or some sort of disease, thirty percent of the time it is a structural or accidental issue - they have been cut, bumped, broken a bone, or something like that is going on; thirty percent of the time it is a chemical issue where they are out of balance in their internal chemistry; and then thirty percent of all patients present to physicians with conditions that they have developed due to an emotional issue or energetic blockage.

The energy therapies that relate to this philosophy focus on clearing and neutralizing the emotional charge that is underlying many individuals' physical pain, emotional issues, depression, phobias, and addictions. Often times the dis-ease itself is just a prolonged situation with an underlying emotional issue. The value is in the fact that most energy psychology, energy medicine, energy therapy modalities approach the client or patient in a WHOLE-istic manner, looking at all aspects of that person's life, health, well-being as part of the basic treatment.[9]

For many of us who are not "physicians", but who function as health and wellness facilitators or coaches and therapists, there are many tools, techniques, modalities that when used, may fall under the category of "Energy Therapy".

I like what Dr. Scott Walker said about energy therapy as he shared why he developed Neuro Emotional Technique over twenty-five years ago:

"In a state of frustration, insecurity and, thankfully, *curiosity*, NET (Neuro Emotional Technique) was eventually developed. Initially I felt frustrated because some patients got well, while others didn't. I also felt insecure because I didn't have a satisfying answer for myself or my patients who asked as to

---

[9] For more information visit: http://www.netmindbody.com/for-patients/an-explanation-of-net

why their conditions didn't respond or why they kept coming back. I was curious, however, and my search took me to "stress" and the body's conditioned emotional reaction to stress. The interesting thing was I, through reading neuroscience articles, found the emotional response to be *physiologically* based and not psychologically based! That was lucky, because I don't know very much about psychology, and I was not about to make a career out of talking, talking, and more talking to patients about their problems! Please save me from that! On the other hand, we, as chiropractors, are well versed in dealing with physiology. In a nutshell, NET works by having the patient think-feel about their pain/issue while a special vertebral adjustment is given." Scott Walker, D.C.[10]

With recent discoveries proving that most of the neuro-physiology, psychology, neurology, and neuro-linguistics studies of the past are out-of-date, there is much validation now to approaching "healing" from a

---

[10] Walker, Scott - *The American Chiropractor*, December 2008, pg. 18 http://amchiropractor.com

meridian-based tapping technique or hands-on energy therapy point of view.

The old concept that emotional pain is separate from physical pain has been proven incorrect by many researchers and practitioners. We now see clearly the direct mind-body connection, and can target our modalities toward the mind/emotional components in order to ease stress there and also support the health of the physical body.

The old approach of using talk therapies to approach emotional and psychological pain has been questioned now since neuroscience studies are proving that emotional responses are *physiologically* based and not psychologically based! It would make sense that the best coach, therapist, wellness facilitator would get more success from approaching emotional and psychological issues through accessing the physiology, or physical body's electro-magnetic field rather than using traditional therapies that approach the same problems psychologically through the left brain.

Many traditional therapists have aligned themselves with EMDR techniques, hypnotherapy, acupuncture in order to offer more successful interventions, and the meridian tapping techniques seem to combine the best aspects of all of these in easy-to-use and easy-to-teach packages that go deeper into clearing neuro-pathways of discomfort from emotions.

A practitioner may choose from a variety of modalities including Neuro Emotional Technique / NET, Emotional Freedom Techniques / EFT, Reiki, Healing Touch, Touch for Health, EMDR, Applied and Educational Kinesiology, Eden Energy Medicine approaches, Thought Field Therapy / TFT, among many others. These are easily introduced into on-going practices of medicine, chiropractic, naturopathy, psychology, hypnotherapy, massage therapy, acupuncture, coaching, and others. And, the benefits are unlimited in that by clearing the root causes of dis-ease, the various treatments usually offered in each discipline become more beneficial and bring about faster results in helping the body, mind, spirit to heal.

Before finding EFT, I developed an energy de-charging technique that I labeled **The Cuztic Resistance Clearing Process**, and I now share that in a guidebook form that is available on my blog.[11]

The Cuztic technique is somewhat similar to concepts involved in the EMDR method, in Educational Kinesiology, and in Dr. Pat Carrington's "Choices Method". The process invites you to identify an issue around which you feel stress. You are guided to create polar opposites of the best scenario and worst scenario. Then you alternate thinking of each of these issue polarities as you move your eyes in a variety of directions and access parts of your brain. You may go to the link above to download your complimentary copy of the book.

I have enjoyed using the Cuztic process, as it is a potent neutralizer of emotional charge. This is a

---

[11] To access the e-book go to: http://AlchemistAnne.com

handy tool to utilize when you are stressed when making a decision. The process will help you feel neutral about any of the outcomes that you place into the process, and without emotional charge you can easily make your decision.

Over the years I have found that meridian-based tools like NET and EFT are very efficient, easy, and pain-free ways to help clients or patients immediately shift the energy around any emotional or psychological blockage and move forward. Practitioners find it exciting to share a potent tool that can change a person's life, especially when they have been struggling with emotional issues blocking life progress and are reluctant to revisit the old trauma or experience that is the root of the issue. Using a meridian-based energy therapy modality is usually so easy, quick, and painless, that it seems almost like a miracle to some people to feel the relief after the emotional charge has been cleared. This is why I integrated energy therapy into my coaching practice years ago; I wanted to be able to go deeper with my clients, and also give them tools so that they wouldn't become dependent on me.

There are many coaches and therapists, as well as all other kinds of health and wellness facilitators who are beginning to apply energy therapy modalities in their practices. We can all benefit from applying or receiving Energy Therapy treatments for whatever causes imbalance or pain of any area of our lives.

Are you ready to discover the benefits of Energy Therapy in your life and practice?

SUCCESSFULLY ACCESSING THE SUBCONSCIOUS MIND

When we consider how our mind functions, we each have two hemispheric personalities which not only think about things differently, but they process emotions and carry our bodies in different ways.

The right mind brain feels the whole picture of life in the present NOW state, and sees the connectedness of all. It has the enthusiasm and wonder of a child and it sees beyond each person's seemingly "separateness" from the rest of creation. This right hemispheric mind smiles a lot and is extremely friendly. It feels rather than analyzes, and it plays many important roles for us.

The right mind helps us to feel the sensations of our senses and it is a portal for the richness of life. It is filled with gratitude, is content, compassionate, nurturing, and intrinsically optimistic. It helps us to create energetically, and it connects us with the planet and all other beings. It is our intuitive self, our curious child, and the seat of our Divine Self – the wise person and observer. It connects us to the universal abundance and protects us from being hurt emotionally.

It is also like a sponge soaking up all from the environment and keeping tabs on anything that feels dangerous or unsafe. Any small ripple in the smooth seas of its perceived reality is encoded for future reference, and then automatically a protection shield is placed up so that we never have to be bothered by that ripple again. This is what often, years later, might come back to haunt us as we find re-curring negative cycles, inner blocks creating self-sabotage, and illness creeping into our lives.

In contrast, our left hemispheric analytical mind is preoccupied with details and runs our lives on tight schedules. It produces our more serious side. It makes decisions based on past consciously-remembered experiences, defines boundaries, and judges everything as right or wrong, good or bad. It makes up stories based on whatever data it can gather – and even if the information is not complete... it still comes to a conclusion. It causes us to worry about things that the right lobe & limbic subconscious brain doesn't seem to be worried about... even if the cause of the inner challenge is actually held in the subconscious.

Our brain hemispheres do an intricate dance to help us survive and make sense of life around us. The right mind inputs new insight in every moment to update old files containing outdated information. Our left mind makes judgments based on data and past experience. Often we become "possessed" by our left mind judgments and refuse to open our eyes wider to allow our right mind to re-calibrate the data in order for us to open to a new belief. In these cases we have made a decision that we are attached to forever. And, the left mind doesn't really help this situation because it continues to insist that it is right – based on its data – and refuses to open to new possibilities from the "open-minded" right mind.

The phrase "thinking out of the box" describes the right mind normal activity. The "box" was created by the left mind as it learned, analyzed, and created structure for the way something was "supposed" to be. The right mind would much rather be free to create and try something new.

A major role of the subconscious right lobe and limbic mind is to protect us, and it sees the world in a very wholistic manner. If we are treading into uncharted territory; or if we are going into a place in life where we've been before and where we got hurt, upset, or something traumatic happened, our subconscious mind will block us even though our left mind is analyzing, planning, positioning, and setting up action steps to take. We just won't be able to move forward if our subconscious is in protection mode.

Meridian Tapping Techniques address the perceived confusion between the hemispheres and access the right mind through the electro-magnetic biofield using meridian points that are the same points as have been used in acupressure and acupuncture for thousands of years. In my work I often refer to the right mind as our "subconscious" because we tend to consider our left mind to be our "conscious" thoughts, beliefs, operating system.

In accessing this innermost creative subconscious child-like aspect inside of each of us there are specific "best practice" ways to do so.

Children get scared easily – so does our subconscious. We must speak kindly and gently to our innermost self in order for it to listen to us.

Children often get confused when we use negative semantics such as no, not, don't, won't, etc. They pick up the main verbs, nouns, adjectives and might get confused about the extra word thrown in with the main details. Our subconscious hears the positive words in our verbal communication and tends to negate the negatives. So, when we speak to our subconscious mind it is best to create statements that use only words in their positive forms. We can still introduce negative topics or issues, but will just word them using positive phrasing.

The subconscious mind thinks kinesthetically in feelings, colors, sensory responses, so talk to it so that it understands, and remember that typical analytical mind messages of mere data might not be as understandable to the right mind as messages with feeling.

Using the EFT Set-up Statement

In EFT / Emotional Freedom Techniques, I highly respect Gary Craig for putting together the original basic set-up statement so that the subconscious will listen.[12]

The classic set-up is a strong, balanced affirmation statement. Starting with **"Even though..."** plus adding the issue you would like to bring the intention to, the statement is non-threatening, in the now, and

---

[12] For more information visit: http://emofree.com

usually states a feeling or situation that exists. The second part of the statement: **"I deeply and completely accept myself,"** reinforces to the right mind that it is not being threatened, and that, in fact, it is being appreciated for who it is – now.

If a client feels resistant to using the second part of the set-up statement it is probably because their mind has created a belief that they are not worthy to be appreciated or loved. This is a perfect opportunity for an EFT facilitator to help that person clear that old belief before they get any farther into using energy therapy. In initially clearing the set-up statement many other issues may disappear as well.

What the set-up statement actually does is:
1. In the first part it accentuates the issue that you would like to clear and let go of. This could be a condition, a fear, a re-occurring life cycle that you would really like to shift out of your life.
2. The second part of the statement is an affirmation acknowledging that you are okay,

that yes you are not perfect, you do have your good, bad, and ugly, but you accept yourself. You accept the fact that you aren't perfect, and that you are just the way you are and that's okay for now. It's okay because you are evolving, you are moving forward, and you are getting better every day.

When I facilitate an EFT session I start out with the set-up statement teamed with the "karate chop" small intestine meridian point on the side of the hand – just as Gary Craig instructs us in classical EFT. In very difficult cases of long or chronic patterns or disease I start with the upper rib cage "sore spots" or an additional tapping area including the thymus and heart center points. While tapping I have the client focus on the feeling of the issue to be dissolved. Then we move to the karate chop point with the set-up statement. This usually gets the subconscious on track so that we don't have to address psychological reversal. (This will be addressed later.)

The balance in that statement enables your subconscious limbic mind, that little child whose job it is to protect you from being hurt, scared, traumatized in ways that you have been emotionally impacted in the past, to easily start paying attention without feeling threatened in any way. It hears about the issue at hand and feels the words of encouragement in the second half of the statement. With this balanced statement not only are you sharing your concern about the issue with your subconscious, but you are also saying, "don't let me scare you too much, it's okay, I recognize that you are doing the best you can do, and I really, really appreciate all that you are doing." If you came in with a statement that was just stating the issue you wish to get rid of, and you were bombarding your sensitive right mind subconscious with just the negatives, then it would be intimidated, and might not want to respond, but instead might go more strongly into protection mode.

When Meridian Tapping Techniques Won't Work

I won't go into a lot of detail here, but sometimes our electromagnetic field gets confused and we become "switched". This apolaria or psychologically reversed condition, where yes means no, no means yes, black means white, white means black, can be brought on through dehydration, an allergic reaction chemically, long-term chronic pain or depression, a trauma to the system, or simply the fear of the subconscious mind when it is approached and asked to look at an upsetting emotional issue.

No matter what the intention is or how well one facilitates EFT, if a person is switched off, his/her subconscious and electromagnetic field will not accept any kind of energy therapy, and will not provide accurate answers to any muscle-testing that may be added to the EFT protocol. In order to save time and energy some action must be taken to remedy the situation at the point where the practitioner notices that no progress to de-charge the issue is being made.

There are a variety of ways that the condition of apolaria or psychological reversal may be remedied.

- In EFT we repeat the set-up statement at least three times while rubbing "sore spots" (which are actually neuro-lymphatic points) on the upper chest/rib cage, or tapping the karate chop points while stating the set-up statement. (This point that accesses the small intestine meridian can relate to emotions dealing with feeling lost & vulnerable, abandoned, deserted, insecure, lacking love, muddled thinking, confusion, depleted, suppressed, absent minded, sluggish memory. Can you understand why this point may be potently used to bring the frightened and confused subconscious mind back to listen to what you have to say?)
- In NET the doctors of chiropractic can perform a cervical adjustment at C1, while the rest of us can apply a homeopathic remedy that is formulated especially for the apolarity issue.[13]

---

[13] For more information visit:
http://www.netmindbody.com/for-patients/homeopathic-remedy-support

- Some acupuncturists find that holding your arms together – inner wrist-to-wrist will complete a circuit and remedy the energetic flow in the field.
- In Naturopathy two techniques include:
    - Tap all 10 fingertips at the thymus point in the upper middle chest on sternum, or
    - Cross your arms and place together the thumb, index, and middle fingers of each hand and touch on the outer ends of the eyebrows, then cross the other way (upper arm under lower, etc.).

So, with this in mind, as I perform EFT I feel it is important to tap the karate chop point while using a good strong set-up statement stated three times at the beginning of each round – especially in group tapping – in order to ensure that all of the right minds in the group are able to switch into "feeling mode" and can pay attention to the work we are doing.

I also stress that feeling the emotion of the issue and holding the "snapshot" of an original event while tapping is vitally more important than focusing on the words that are used. (I do not address Post Traumatic Stress cases in this same way; that is another report.)

So, with the understanding that the subconscious mind is truly in charge and the analytical left brain mind is only about 2% "conscious" of all that is going on around it, you can see how important it is to understand how to access the subconscious right mind and work directly with it to clear inner resistance, emotional charge, and other blockages to peace, love, joy, health in life!

Respecting the Body's Priorities

Often people use meridian tapping with a specific goal in mind. And, sometimes there are the "one minute miracles" where the issue is just bubbling at the top and ready to be cleared forever. Other times, however, the specific goal is not met in one, two, several sessions... and usually when this happens the person starts to realize other shifts in their consciousness, perception, attitudes, level of pain, sense of self, etc.

It is my assertion that meridian tapping ALWAYS works, however, it works on clearing the body's own priorities... in the order directed by the body, subconscious, and biofield. In NET we use an on-line questionnaire based on frequency of physical symptoms to tell us practitioners where to start. The most symptomatic meridians are usually the ones that need the work first, and after they are serviced, then the next layer rises to the surface, and so on until each layer is peeled off and not only is the person's specific goal met, but there are many other benefits experienced in the process.

Working with the meridians is an almost magical experience because so much can be accomplished in so little time... in all areas of one's being.

It can be noted here that if a practitioner tries to WILL that personal priority issue to clear instead of allowing the body to naturally get there when ready, that the issues that seem to be cleared will come back, and success may seem short-lived.

It is also now known via research and testing that when a person has emotional blockages and inner resistance, that nutrition is not as well absorbed, medicines have stronger negative side effects, chiropractic adjustments don't hold as well, acupuncture and acupressure treatments are not as potent, and life just does not flow as well. But, on the flip side, when the underlying issues are cleared... in the priority preferred by the body, then the opposite of all of the mentioned issues is true..., so nutrition helps the body, meds are beneficial with fewer dangers, chiropractic and acu-treatments are more successful and potent, and all other wellness-related interventions work better with greater results.

I suppose that the message here is to have patience in the process and allow your body to call the shots and to bring up the bigger issues to work on first, getting to others in due time.

TIPS FOR NURTURING YOUR SUBCONSCIOUS

Now that you better realize the sensitivity yet strength of your subconscious and energy field, here are some tips to remember as you perform any process that accesses the electro-magnetic biofield via meridians, and allows you to communicate directly with this special part of yourself.

1. **Respect your subconscious and treat it gently.** When this first point is difficult it is a good indicator that you must address the inner critical voice. So often we are our own worst critics and judges, and that only clouds the issue with more stress.

2. **Be very clear in your communication to your subconscious.** Sometimes muddled thinking or inarticulate communication is a good indicator of the underlying issue.

3. **Repeat to yourself as though you were speaking to a child.** If this brings up agitation, anger, impatience, then tap them away.

4. **Be patient with this complicated and sensitive part of your mind & being. It is looking at whatever you are showing it and fighting off the analytical mind in order to best process the data in its own terms and decide whether to accept it or not.** If the analytical mind seems to be "going crazy" with too much mind chatter, then tap between the two eyebrows, above the nose on the 3rd eye point and breathe out the stress until your mind quiets.

5. **Approach your subconscious mind with a loving open heart. Never thrust your negative emotion at it – instead explain lovingly the change that you desire.** Beware of the critical inner voice – it can be mean and

chase the sensitive subconscious back into hiding.

6. **Slow down your energy and pace. Your subconscious is not in a hurry even though your left mind may be late.** Breathing disciplines such as yoga, prana yama, etc. might support you to bring more "allowing" energy into your field.

7. **Be in the NOW. Focus on the present and communicate what is NOW rather than focusing on past or future. The issue or condition that you wish to clear is bothering you now, even if it did occur for the first time in the past.** A daily practice of meditation is wonderful for bringing you into the NOW.

8. **Encourage your subconscious mind to be there with you, and encourage it to help you to let go of the unnecessary issue or charge related to it.** When you show respect

to your subconscious mind it will work more closely with you – and it is SO MUCH MORE POWERFUL than the left brain analytical mind! When it feels safe it starts to provide information for clearing.

9. **Connect with your subconscious mind. Talk to it. Assure it that you know it is inside of you working hard.** This is the part of you that is running over 98% of your reality, so make it your friend and ally!

10. **Speak gently to your right mind subconsicous – never yell at it – even if that is done silently "in your mind".** Control that critical voice and purge those old recordings, negative beliefs, and other demons that are abusive to your still inner self.

11. **Protect your subconscious mind by resisting negative outside influences – TV, news, violence, etc.** Whatever you react to emotionally is considered to be your own "real"

experience by your subconscious and electro-magnetic field. You will carry the terror, pain, anger, frustration, etc. from a dark movie, book, story from a friend, etc. Keep your space clear and shield yourself from negative energies... as you remember to daily clear your field!

12. **Drink plenty of water so that you don't become switched off or apolar.** Especially when doing energy work it is necessary to drink much more water than usual. Imagine yourself to be a large battery that will burn up inside without water to cool and hydrate it. Dehydration feels horrible, so don't go there!

13. **Speak about feelings rather than thoughts to your right mind.** Your right mind communicates through feelings, pictures, colors, shapes, textures. Whenever you catch yourself focusing on words rather than the feelings while doing an EFT process, push yourself back to the feelings or else wait until

later for the tapping protocol, because just words and taps will NOT get the results that you desire!

14. **Trust that your subconscious is always working hard on the job – seemingly too hard at times!** The subconscious mind and energy field handles keeping you alive and running at least 98% of the body-mind-spirit show. Would you give all of your power to someone who knew only 2% of what was going on? So, don't give all the power and credence to your left brain just because it loves to solve problems, make decisions, and worry!

15. **In using energy therapy tools, break issues into separate manageable pieces rather than putting everything together. Focus specifically on one issue at a time.** You wouldn't eat a whole cake in one bite. You wouldn't tell a child every step in a long process all at once. Break your issues into specific separate aspects so that they clear more

easily... and try to go back to the original event in the case of a re-occurring pattern or cycle.

16. **Communicate clearly that you are clearing certain negative or unwanted issues and adding aspects of your life or outcomes that you do desire.** I focus specifically on certain words when I facilitate N-hanced EFT with my clients. I do not use the following words: "release", "want", negatives, among others. I do enjoy using more powerful words placed into positive sentences: "clear", "let go of", "dissolve", "choose", "intend", "allow", among others.

17. **Patiently work with the wording of set-up statements until you identify the top priority issue that is up for you. You may also use muscle-testing or some other energetic measuring process to identify the top priority that the subconscious mind can most easily let go of in the moment,... and know that these energetic priorities**

can and do shift. The body has its own priority of which issues it will clear first, second, etc. In NET I ask the body using kinesiology, if there was an original event related to the issue at hand. The body always knows and tells me so that we can clear the earliest event and that, then clears all subsequent events in the cycle or pattern. In EFT one can surmise intuitively or look for the patterns and cycles that are obvious. In my practice we clear a lot of DNA issues from ancestors.

18. **Reinforce that your subconscious is doing a great job. Thank it and encourage it to come out and play.** Gratitude is a wonderful vibrational booster and it also encourages more good energy and cooperation! I often tap the top of the head or the thymus point at the center of the frontal rib cage while expressing gratitude to the subconscious.

19. **Visualize the outcome that you desire – complete with sense-oriented, detailed**

scenario description (in writing is best) that can help guide your subconscious mind in the direction that you desire. Let your feelings guide you to that which you most desire! Daily focus on the feelings of what you want and soon you will discover that you are living that life!

20. **Love your wonderful mind – both right and left hemispheres, and all of the rest of it – for all that it does for you. Share the gratitude!** Balance is so important! So, enjoy this human experience more as you utilize the many energy therapy techniques available to you!

ENERGY CLEARING AFTER A TAPPING SESSION

Over the years I have learned that after a major energy clearing process has been performed, there is often some energetic residue or what I call "ash" left in the area surrounding wherever the energy process was performed. I recognize and feel this residue, so I always urge my clients to take some steps to dispel this energetic "ash" so that they can be fully free of the hold of the issue that has been cleared.

To better understand this concept you might look at a couple of analogies:

- When one is performing a physical cleanse a substance may be taken that will enable toxins to be released from the body. Drinking lots of water will assist the lymph glands and the intestinal track to better wash out the toxins still remaining in the body. There is a need for some cleansing agent to flush out the refuse.

- In the case of an amputee there are often reports that an individual can still "feel" the limb or digit that has been removed. In our case the cleared energy may be outside of the body's electro-magnetic field, but it may still be lingering around the aura, the proximity, the home, car, area most frequented by the person who just purged the energy. Scott Walker calls this "body memory".

When I work with a client I make certain suggestions of what they need to do to cleanse themselves, their living area, their working area, their car, their jewelry, their general surroundings in order to be free of the old energies that they have cleared with EFT or NET or another energy therapy tool.

Dispelling the Energetic "Ash" after an EFT Session

For several years I have been aware of an energetic cloud or state that seemed to provide static in the environment after a "Tapping Summit" had offered a week of daily EFT tapping sessions via internet with tens of thousands of people world-wide in attendance. For at least two days after the event ended I felt some definite energy static in the environment. When I asked others if they had felt it, many reported that they had. My personal opinion is that after so many people came together for 7-10 days and tapped out all kinds of issues together world-wide, that the energetic "ash" was hanging in the atmosphere and took a few days to clear naturally. This is my opinion based on past experience with energy modalities and the energetic residues that can be left when emotional issues are cleared.

After major clearing sessions using NET or EFT or other meridian tapping processes I normally instruct my clients to make a conscious effort of clearing the energetic "ash" or residue so that they receive quicker results without a feeling of energetic "hang-over". I usually suggest the following easy processes that work quickly:

- In NET we ask the body if it needs a specific homeopathic for this process.
- Take a bath using Epsom salts. Submerge your whole body including your head for best results. This will cleanse your aura and might rid you of some aches and pains in the process.
- Stand under a shower with the intention of cleansing your aura.
- Smudge the space where you performed the meridian tapping by using a smudge stick, stick of incense, or simply walk all around that area with a lighted candle and the intention of clearing out all energetic residue that belongs elsewhere. (You may be amazed at the intuitive insights that you receive as you do this procedure as memories, experiences, etc. that happened in the space you are smudging rush

into your mind. This validates that you are, indeed, cleaning the energy of the space so that you don't walk right back into the energetic cloud that you just let go of in the energy therapy procedure.)
- Remember to smudge your car or any other space where you may have performed an energy-clearing process or where you might have had an encounter or experience that brought up the emotional issue that you cleared.
- Be aware that your jewelry picks up energy. Crystals (including gemstones) are magnifiers, so if they have been around you during an emotional experience or an energy clearing, then they need to be cleansed of that energy debris too. You may intentionally wash them under water to clear away the old unbeneficial energies or you may set them in direct sunlight for a few hours with the intention of cleansing.
- And, make it a practice to clear yourself at least once per day of any energetic "cling-ons" that you might have picked up as you come into

contact with others or outside stimuli. There are many ways to do this easily, including some mentioned above.

My recommendation is that every time you do a deep energy clearing session using a meridian tapping technique, that you intentionally do some clearing of the residue after the process. It is my experience that as a result:

1- The tapping results show up sooner,
2- You will feel more relaxed as your energy shifts and your right mind subconscious makes its shifts in perception,
3- It will be easier for your left mind to move forward with new ideas and beliefs if it is not picking up on old energetic patterns and body memory.
4- Your energy space will feel lighter and more supportive of the conscious transformation you are initiating in your life.

RESOURCES

These are just a few of many great specialists and their works that relate to energy therapy, energy psychology, energy medicine, quantum physics, neuroscience, epigenetics, and so much more that you should look for to deepen your understanding of what you are doing so that you can better Manage Your Energy!

Feinstein, David; Eden, Donna; Craig, Gary: **The Promise of Energy Psychology – Revolutionary Tools for Dramatic Personal Change**, Penguin Group, NY, 2005. Going back to the EFT and Energy Medicine sources, this compilation of discussion and practical techniques is a must-have for all serious energy psychologists.

Lipton, Bruce H.: **The Biology of Belief – Unleashing the Power of Consciousness, Matter, and Miracles,** Elite Books, CA, 2005. This stem-cell biologist explains how the mind, body, and spirit come together and are affected by environment as they attempt to create the life of your desires. Science finally connects with energy!

Oschman, James L.: **Energy Medicine – The Scientific Basis,** Churchill Livingstone Press, NY, 2000. Let's go more deeply into the science of energy!.

Taylor, Jill Bolte: **My Stroke of Insight – A Brain Scientist's Personal Journey**, Viking Penguin Press, 2008. A very good and understandable book that will provide you with more background understanding of your brain, neuroscience, and how your right brain/ subconscious works. It is highly recommended!

I wish you the best as you apply these ENERGY CLEARING TIPS!

If you enjoyed this book, then you may also wish to check out our various books, guides, or recording packages included in our Comprehensive Products & Programs[14] collection at www.ArielaGroup.com .

---
[14] Go to:
http://www.arielagroup.com/products/self_study.php

www.ingramcontent.com/pod-product-compliance
Lightning Source LLC
Chambersburg PA
CBHW061252040426
42444CB00010B/2364